JUST LOOK AT...

LAKE AND RIVER PEOPLES

Terry Jennings

Macdonald Educational

Factual Advisor: Dr. Christopher Green

Editor: Peter Harrison
Teacher Panel: Steve Harley, Anne Merriman,
Joanne Waterhouse
Designer: Ewing Paddock
Production: Rosemary Bishop
Picture Research: Diana Morris

The Publishers would like to thank Survival
International for their assistance in the preparation
of this book.

Illustrations
Peter Bull Cover cartoon, 8–9, 10–11, 12–13, 28,
34–35, 38, 42
S. Pallent/M. Mundy 16, 20(R), 22–23, 32–33,
36–37
Jerry Collins, 14, 18, 20(L), 22, 24, 30, 32

Photographs
Aerofilms: 27
BPCC/Aldus Archive: 14
Robert Harding Picture Library: title page, 11, 39T
Himalayan Images/D. Henderson: 25B
Hoa-Qui/M. Huet: 34
Thomas d'Hoste: 26
Hutchison Picture Library: 12, 13, 17T, 19B
Impact/Homer Sykes: 20, 21
David Keith Jones: 15, 30, 31
MacQuitty International Photographic Collection:
42
MARKA: 19T
Newcastle Central Library: 17B
South American Pictures/Robert Francis: 33
TASS: 36
ZEFA: cover, 8, 23, 29, 35, 39B, 41, 43

Title page photo: Traditional way of catching fish
in a river in Thailand

British Library Cataloguing in Publication Data

Jennings, Terry
    Lake and river peoples.——(Just look at)
    1. Lakes——Juvenile literature——2. Rivers
    —Juvenile literature
    I. Title   II. Series
    551.48   GB1603.8

ISBN 0-356-13215-3

How to use this book
Look first in the contents page to see if the subject you want is listed. For instance, if you want to find out about Burmese peoples, you will find the information on pages 24 and 25. The word list explains the more difficult terms found in this book. The index will tell you how many times a particular subject is mentioned and whether there is a picture of it.

Lake and River Peoples is one of a series of books on how people live. All the books on this subject have an orange colour band around the cover. If you want to know more about how people live, look for other books with an orange colour band in the **Just Look At . . .** series.

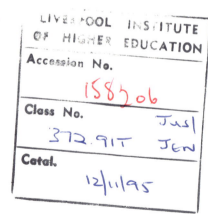
A MACDONALD BOOK
© Macdonald & Co. (Publishers) Ltd 1987

First published in Great Britain in 1987
by Macdonald & Co. (Publishers) Ltd
London & Sydney

Printed in Great Britain by Purnell Book Production Limited.
Member of the BPCC Group.

Macdonald & Co. (Publishers) Ltd
Greater London House, Hampstead Road, London NW1 7QX

CONTENTS

FOOD AND WATER

All living things, including people, must have water to survive. Sometimes this water comes from the sea or from wells. Mostly though, it comes from rivers and lakes.

Many of the world's early civilizations grew up in valleys through which large rivers flowed: in the Nile valley, on the land between the Tigris and Euphrates rivers, in the Indus valley of what is now Pakistan, and in the valley of the Yellow River in China. These five rivers are all very large and they flood regularly.

Although unexpected floods can cause damage and loss of life, all floods carry alluvium, or fine particles of silt and clay, and leave it on the valley floors when the flood goes down. The alluvium makes a very fertile soil in which crops grow well. All rivers deposit some alluvium, but really large ones like the Nile and Yellow rivers have built up huge fertile plains and deltas, and continue to add thin layers of alluvium every time they flood. It was only rivers as large as these which could produce enough food to allow large numbers of people to stay in the same place continuously, and build the first cities.

People living near lakes and rivers also use the water to drink, wash, cook and for other domestic needs. Fish from the lake or river provide an easily obtainable food, and large lakes and rivers also provide a cheap and convenient way of transporting people and their goods.

Source

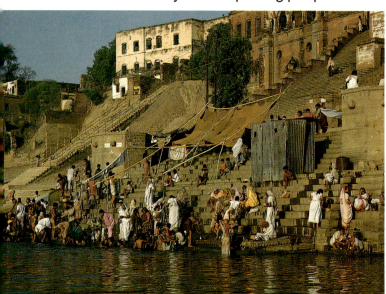

Rice is the main food for almost half the world's peoples. Most rice is grown on the deltas and floodplains of large rivers. ▶

◀ Rivers have religious meaning for some peoples. Hindus bathe in the River Ganges to wash away sin and disease because they believe the river is holy.

Tributary

◀ The Yellow River in China begins in Tibet, and its waters are coloured by the yellow rocks and soil which it flows across in the middle of China. The river ends in a very large delta. ▼

Delta

Floodplain

Meander

Sea

Early Peoples

Archaeologists now believe that the earliest human beings lived in Africa, probably in the area which now includes the Rift Valley and Lake Victoria, more than two million years ago. There is plenty of evidence, from the fossil remains of plants and animals, that in those days East Africa was much wetter and more fertile than it is today.

These early peoples learned to make weapons and tools of stone, bone, ivory, wood and horn. They hunted and killed animals for food, but also ate nuts, seeds, fruits and other parts of plants.

The first domestic animals
Over thousands of years, people in the Middle East discovered how they could improve their food supply. They found that if they burned down trees and shrubs, grass grew quickly in the space that was left. This provided food for wild goats, sheep and other animals which ate grass.

So these wild animals no longer wandered away to find fresh grass, but stayed near the clearings and people. The people did not have to go in search of wild animals to hunt and kill, or follow herds from one place to another. They could stay in one place, living in huts in the clearings they had made.

Water and crops
About 10 000 years ago, people began to farm the land in what has been called the 'Fertile Crescent' in the Middle East. The soils in this area were made fertile by regular floods from the Tigris and Euphrates rivers.

Irrigation
To control the flooding, and to make sure the floodwaters enriched the largest possible area, the people around the Tigris and Euphrates developed irrigation. They dug ditches which allowed water to reach the drier areas of soil farther away from the rivers.

◀ Civilizations which grew up around large rivers extended far beyond the rivers themselves.
A. The Fertile Crescent in 2000 BC.
B. The Indian Empire of Asoka around AD 250.
C. The Chinese Shang Empire around 1000 BC. The small boats are the kinds used by these civilizations.

500 1000
kilometres

N

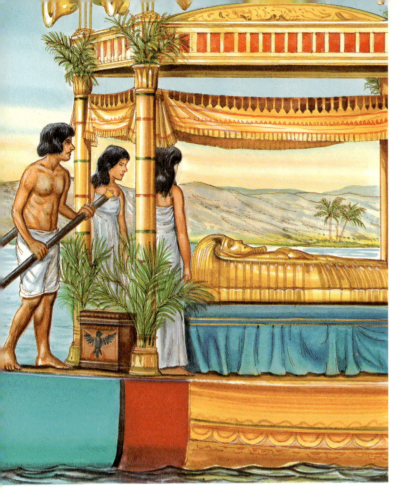

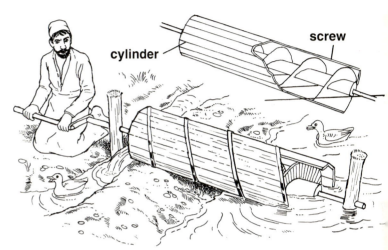

◄ Rivers and boats were important in the funeral customs of many ancient civilizations. The bodies of the Pharaohs, the kings of ancient Egypt, were carried in boats to their tombs, the Pyramids.

The Archimedean screw was one of the earliest irrigation machines. It moves water when someone turns the handle of the screw inside the cylinder. It was used in ancient Egypt to raise water from the river to the river bank, and is still in use in Egypt today. ▼

cylinder

screw

The first civilization
In the river valleys with their fertile floodplains, large quantities of crops could now be grown, which could in turn provide food for a large number of people. With a regular supply of food, the people could stay in one place and build houses. The early villages grew, and, as hundreds of years passed, the world's first towns and cities grew up. For the first time ever, large groups of people were all living together in one place. This allowed people to develop many different skills to provide for the needs of a large community.

People were no longer simply hunters or herders; some could farm, others could trade, and others could make tools or be architects, artists or builders of palaces and temples.

The Sumerians
The world's first city civilization, that of the Sumerians, developed on the fertile strip of land between the Tigris and Euphrates rivers 7000 to 4000 years ago. The Sumerians' many achievements included developing the art of writing, and the crafts of metalworking and making pots out of clay.

▲ These people are fishing in the River Jorhale in India using methods which have hardly changed since before the time of Asoka's Empire.

Along the Zaire

The Zaire river, which was known as the Congo, is the second longest river in Africa after the Nile. Most big rivers are like the Zaire. They have their beginnings in hills or mountains and then flow down, increasing in size as they go, until they reach the sea. The Zaire begins in Zambia, in the highlands between Lake Tanganyika and Lake Malawi. In its narrower, upper reaches the Zaire is calm in places, and boats can travel on it. Other stretches have dangerous rapids and waterfalls.

The Middle Zaire

The Zaire plunges down a series of rapids at Boyoma Falls, just north of the Equator, and then becomes a very wide, slow-moving river again. Here the river is 13 kilometres wide in places, while the lowlands on either side are more than 1000 kilometres wide. The Zaire floods regularly, producing great marshes, some stretching more than 300 kilometres on each side of the river.

▲ Children inspecting fish traps set in a wooden scaffolding across one of the sections of rapids on the Zaire.

The Zaire flows down from mountains 1400 metres above sea level. It curves across central Africa, through dense rainforests, and finally crosses grasslands before it reaches the Atlantic Ocean. The inset map shows how the river's curving path crosses the Equator twice. ▶

Marshes

Lower Zaire

CONGO

Grassland

Mbandaka
1040

ZAIRE

Kinshasa
480

River Zaire

kilometres from ocean

Atlantic Ocean

Matadi
128

total length of river
4160

Some peoples who live along the Zaire bring their goods to market by boat. ▶

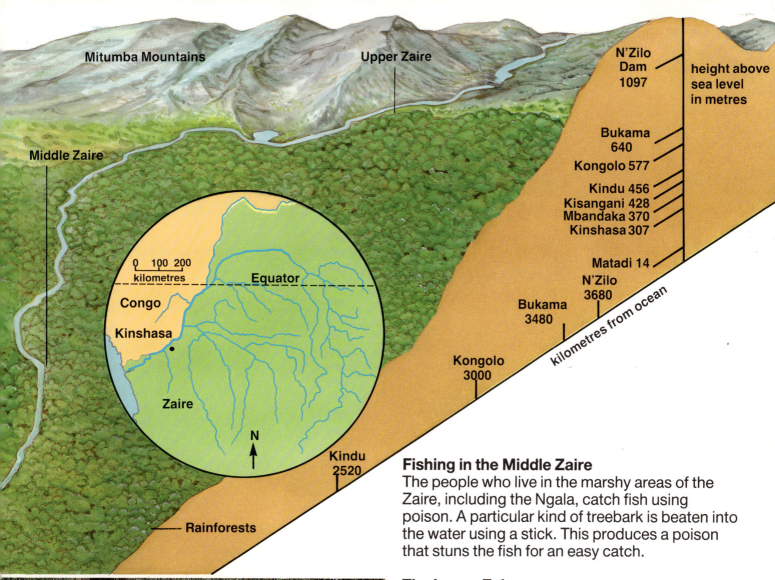

Mitumba Mountains

Upper Zaire

Middle Zaire

N'Zilo Dam 1097

height above sea level in metres

Bukama 640

Kongolo 577

Kindu 456
Kisangani 428
Mbandaka 370
Kinshasa 307

Matadi 14

N'Zilo 3680

Bukama 3480

Kongolo 3000

kilometres from ocean

0   100 200
kilometres

Equator

Congo

Kinshasa

Zaire

N

Kindu 2520

Rainforests

Fishing in the Middle Zaire

The people who live in the marshy areas of the Zaire, including the Ngala, catch fish using poison. A particular kind of treebark is beaten into the water using a stick. This produces a poison that stuns the fish for an easy catch.

The Lower Zaire

About 520 kilometres from the sea, the Zaire enters a long, broad lake, the Malebo Pool, which is about 40 kilometres long and 26 kilometres wide. Kinshasa, the capital of Zaire, is on the south shore, while Brazzaville, the Congo's capital, is on the opposite shore.

The Lower Zaire then begins its descent by rapids to the Atlantic Ocean. Some of the river's energy has been harnessed at Inga in a giant hydro-electric power station which supplies electricity for Kinshasa. Finally the river slows down again as it enters its huge estuary and meets the waters of the Atlantic Ocean.

It is difficult to build roads of any length in the Zaire basin because the area is full of mosquitoes which bite anyone trying to build, and give them malaria and other diseases. This is why the river is so valuable for trade and communication to 25 million people of Zaire and the Congo.

Living on Lakes

Lakes are large areas of fresh or salt water which have land all the way round them. They lie in hollows in the surface of the Earth, and some are very large, like the Great Lakes of North America, which are larger than the United Kingdom. The Caspian Sea and the Aral Sea are really lakes, although they are called seas because they are so big and their water is salty.

The Great Lakes

The Great Lakes lie along the border between Canada and the United States of America, and there are five of them: Superior, Michigan, Huron, Erie, and Ontario. Originally this area was the home of the Iroquois Indians. They were farmers who also hunted and fished, and lived in villages occupied by several families. They moved on every five to ten years when the soil around the village became exhausted.

Caspian Sea 1

Aral Sea 2

Lake Victoria 3

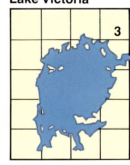

	surface area (square kilometres)
1.	371 000
2.	66 500
3.	68 100
4.	82 414

Lake Superior 4

◀ Chicago's position on the shores of Lake Michigan, close to the Great Plains of the USA, make it a major centre for manufacture and transport. It has been calculated that the water in all the Great Lakes is enough to flood the whole USA to a depth of one full metre.

▲ These are the four largest lakes in the world. The Caspian Sea and the Aral Sea are in the Soviet Union, and both are salt water lakes. Lake Superior, in Canada, and Lake Victoria, in Africa, are fresh-water lakes. In the maps above, each square equals 100 square kilometres.

Cattle drinking in Lake Victoria. Few plants grow in the dry soils around the lake, and cattle often feed on waterweeds. A sailing canoe is passing not far behind the cattle. ▼

Modern Great Lakes

The first Europeans to settle in North America used the Great Lakes as a convenient route into the interior of the continent. The lakes are still an important route for transporting goods inside Canada and the USA. Famous cities such as Chicago, Detroit, Cleveland and Toronto have grown up on their shores. Yet the lakes are also used for sport and recreation, and many national parks have been created along their shores.

From ocean to land

The lakes are joined by natural channels and canals which allow ships to go all the way from the Atlantic Ocean to the ports of Duluth and Superior in the centre of the continent. Every year the lakes and canals freeze over in about mid-December. This brings shipping to a halt for about four months, until the ice thaws again, usually in mid-April.

Lake Victoria

Lake Victoria is Africa's largest lake and, after Lake Superior, the second largest freshwater lake in the world. The many shallows along the shores of Lake Victoria provide ideal breeding conditions for fish. These are a staple diet of the several million people of Uganda, Kenya and Tanzania who live around the lake. Fish were probably also an important food for the earliest human beings whom archaeologists believe lived in this area more than two million years ago.

Shipping on Lake Victoria is important to the local economy, but recent drops in the water level, brought about by drought and the silting up of the lake, have forced a number of ports to close. Lake Victoria is one of the sources of the River Nile. To the north, where the White Nile leaves the lake at Owen Falls, a hydro-electric power station provides electricity for Uganda and Kenya.

RIVER PEOPLES

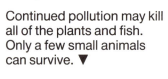

Once many people all over the world relied directly on rivers for their living. Now the world's river peoples are being shown new ideas and standards, new technology and new languages. Thousands of tribes of Indians once lived in the Amazon basin in South America. Over the centuries they have suffered at the hands of colonists looking for gold, and then later from settlers wanting to create plantations of rubber trees. Today people are still trying to change the land where the remaining Indians live. New roads have opened up the forest to developers who want to fell the valuable timber trees, or to extract minerals or set up huge cattle ranches.

The lives of river peoples are changing in the industrialized countries too. The massive shipyards on the River Tyne in northern England, and on the River Clyde in Scotland, are empty. The fall in the world demand for shipping means there is now little demand for new ships such as oil tankers. These changes are not worldwide, however, ship-building is still a major industry in Japan.

Until about 40 years ago London was the largest port in the world. Now cargoes are not carried loose in the holds of ships, but are sent in large containers. The ships which carry these containers now berth at a new container port in the Thames Estuary at Tilbury. The thousands who used to work in the Port of London have had to look for new jobs, while the warehouses are being developed as offices and luxury homes.

Clean rivers and streams contain many plants and animals, including fish of different kinds. ▼

If the water becomes polluted, plants and animals which need most oxygen die first of all. ▼

Continued pollution may kill all of the plants and fish. Only a few small animals can survive. ▼

If the pollution stops, the plants and animals begin to return to live again in the waters of the river. ▼

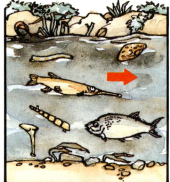

▲ A new road being built across a tributary of the Amazon River at Manaus. The armed guards are protecting the workers from attacks by Indians who are angry at losing their traditional lands.

A Chilean warship, the *General O'Higgins*, being launched at one of the Tyne shipyards around the end of the 19th century, when Newcastle was one of the industrialized world's main ship-building cities. ▶

The Waura

Once thousands of tribes lived in the Amazon basin. The rainforest gave them food and shelter, while the rivers provided fish and a means of travel. Now only about 150 tribes remain, and one of them, the Waura, live in a national park, the Xingu Park, south of the River Amazon.

Waura villages

There are less than a hundred Waura. Like many Amazonian peoples, their numbers have been severely reduced by diseases introduced by newcomers to the continent. They live in a village of large huts called *malocas*, which are made of palm fibres and dry leaves, woven on a framework of poles. Individual Waura tribespeople may own a single cooking pot or drinking jar, some hunting equipment, and the bands of cloth which are their clothes. But they share the land and river where they live, and their work and the food they eat.

Waura children returning to their village in a large clearing in the forest. Two huts, or *malocas*, can be seen in the distance. ▼

▲ A Waura Indian stands in the bow of a dugout canoe using a pole to frighten fish into a net held by a partner in the stern of the canoe.

The Waura live in the Xingu Park, situated by the Xingu River. This is a tributary of the Amazon, the world's second longest river. ▼

South America

Atlantic Ocean

Amazon River

BRAZIL

Amazon River length: 6280 kilometres

N

Xingu Park —

0 100 kilometres

Growing crops

Some of the women grow food in clearings surrounding the village. The main food they grow is mandioca, or cassava, a plant whose underground stems are ground up to make a starchy flour. Other women prepare food in the village, care for the children, or weave hammocks or body bands on simple looms. The women also make pots and animal-shaped bowls from clay they collect on the river banks.

Hunting and fishing

The men spend their days hunting and fishing. After mandioca, the Waura eat more fish than anything else. They also hunt animals in the forest, but mostly after heavy rains have made it difficult for them to catch fish in the swollen rivers.

Sometimes, in the drier parts of the Upper Xingu, they set fire to a small patch of forest. The Waura then kill the monkeys, deer and other animals which run out of the forest to escape the flames, using spears or bows and arrows.

The Xingu Park

Today the Waura number less than a hundred people. Originally their only contact with neighbouring villages was limited to the occasional festival, or to exchanging things they didn't need with people in other villages. The Xingu Park area where the Waura now live was set up in 1961 to protect the Waura and the other tribes of the region when development threatened their traditional lands and ways of life.

The future

Already, however, the Xingu Park has been reduced from its original size and opened up to outsiders by one of the new highways. The Waura now meet and trade regularly with members of the many other tribes in the relatively small area of the Xingu Park. But the Indians in the Park have fought to have their land rights recognized, and the future does not look completely bleak for them. Some of the other Amazon Indians are less happy. Many have turned to begging along the new roads, or in the nearby towns.

The Ma'adan

The Marsh or Ma'adan Arabs live in the part of southern Iraq which is enclosed by the Tigris and Euphrates rivers. This marshland, which is very difficult to reach, is an area where patches of open water are mixed with forests of giant reeds

Island homes

The Marsh Arabs build their houses on small islands. The houses are similar to those of the Marsh Arabs' ancestors, the ancient Sumerians, who lived in this region 7000 years ago. The Marsh Arabs bend rows of thick reed columns and splice them together to form an arched framework. They fasten reed mats to the framework to create the walls and roof of the house. By the side of each house they build a small platform on which the family's water buffaloes can shelter at night.

The animals are called water buffaloes because they love to lie in water or to wallow in mud to keep cool and avoid flies.

The area where the Marsh Arabs live is very close to the border between the modern countries of Iraq and Iran. ▼

Europe
Asia
Africa

IRAN
River Tigris
N
IRAQ
River Euphrates
Persian Gulf

Euphrates River
2700 kilometres long

Tigris River
1850 kilometres long

Arabian Sea

0   100
kilometres

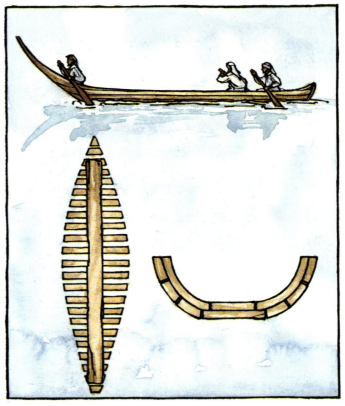

◄ A Marsh Arab reed house on its artificial island of reeds and mud. A water buffalo rests beside it.

A new refrigerator in a Marsh Arab home. *Allah*, the Muslim word for God, is written on the 'fridge door to show its value. Muslims are followers of the prophet Muhammad. ▼

Few of the islands on which the Marsh Arabs build their houses are natural. The people make them by piling together mud and large heaps of reeds which they gather from the marshes. Growing up to six metres in height, the reeds provide food for the livestock, and indirectly for the Marsh Arabs, as well as fuel and material for mats and other woven goods.

Making a living

Most Marsh Arabs live by fishing and keeping water buffaloes. At dawn each day they take the buffaloes to graze on the marshes. They seldom slaughter the buffaloes for their meat, but keep them for their milk and dung. The Marsh Arabs dry the dung and use it as a fuel for the household fires. They drink the buffalo milk fresh or make it into butter or yoghurt.

◄ The Marsh Arabs' high-prowed canoes are made of wood and are carvel-built. This means that the planks are fitted edge to edge. The canoes are waterproofed with a coating of tar.

Boat-building and fishing

Apart from weaving reed mats to sell to the outside world, the other major industry of the Marsh Arabs is boat-building. The design of the canoes has not changed for centuries. The Marsh Arabs use the canoes for both travel and fishing. The marshmen stand in the prows of their canoes when they go out fishing, poised with five-pronged spears held ready to stab at any large fish which swims by.

Changing lifestyles

After hundreds of years without major change, the lives of the Marsh Arabs are in a state of upheaval. One important change which has taken place is that the Iraqi government has provided them with electricity, refrigerators, motor-canoes and money. There is also a school, built from reeds, which is attended by many of the younger children. Previously the children were taught by their parents. Other changes are planned, including flood control and drainage of large areas of the marshes to grow sugar cane. A factory has already been built to produce sugar from the sugar-cane. Other factories are planned which will turn the reeds into paper.

War in the marshes

The war which began between Iraq and Iran in 1981 has also made a lot of changes to how the Marsh Arabs live. In 1984, 1985 and 1986 the Iranian Army launched attacks across the marshland. At times as many as 500 000 troops took part, and many of the Marsh Arabs were killed, while thousands more were wounded or taken prisoner, and their villages were destroyed in the attacks. Large areas of the marshland are now under Iranian control. Even once the war ends, it is now unlikely that the Marsh Arabs will ever be able to resume their old way of life.

Thai River Life

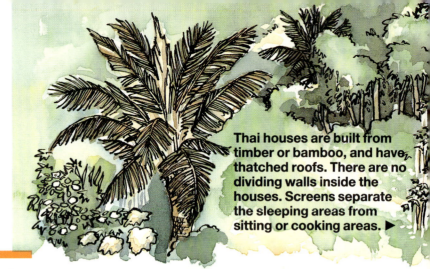

Thai houses are built from timber or bamboo, and have thatched roofs. There are no dividing walls inside the houses. Screens separate the sleeping areas from sitting or cooking areas. ▶

The Central Thai people of Thailand live mostly in the area of the Chao Phraye river basin. On the banks of this river stands the capital of Thailand, Bangkok. It is Thailand's most important port, and also one of the fastest-growing cities in South-East Asia.

Originally Bangkok had almost no roads. Instead the whole city, and most of lowland Thailand, was criss-crossed by canals, or *klongs*. People lived by the side of the *klongs*, and everything they needed was brought to them in wide flat barges. Over the years, many of the *klongs* have been filled in and replaced by roads, especially in Bangkok. Many *klong* dwellers still live in the traditional way, although Bangkok's growth is affecting people in the country.

Houses on stilts

The *klong* dwellers live in houses built of teak or bamboo and raised from the ground by wooden stilts to avoid snakes and flooding. Most of the houses have overhanging thatched roofs, and each has a wooden pier where the family's boat can be tied up. The family uses the area underneath the house for storage, and for sheltering the buffaloes, pigs and poultry.

Using the klongs

The *klong* dwellers use their canals for almost everything, including washing themselves and washing their clothes, and for food, transport and recreation. In the more built-up areas, some of the *klong* dwellers make their living by cultivating a small piece of land behind their homes and selling what they've grown. Others work in the many timber yards along the Chao Phraye and its *klongs*, or run small shops and restaurants. Some *klong* dwellers also own garages which supply petrol for boats' outboard motors.

The Chao Phraye is Thailand's most important river system. It flows into the Gulf of Thailand. ▲

Cleaning out the klongs

From time to time the *klongs* have to be cleaned out. Then one of the families builds two mud walls across the *klong* on either side of its house. That part of the *klong* is emptied using buckets or a pump. The thick mud at the bottom is lifted out by hand and used as a fertilizer on the rice fields.

Rice-growing

Much of the Thai countryside is a vast area of flat fields, *klongs* and villages spreading across the Chao Phraye delta. Only one main crop is grown, which is rice. When the river floods, it enriches the soil. The farmers sell the rice they don't need, or exchange it for other foods.

Fishing

Apart from rice and vegetables, *klong* dwellers mostly eat fish. They catch these with rods, nets, traps and baskets. Often they build a thick bamboo fence across one of the smaller canals. They can then easily catch the fish at the few openings in the fence.

Over-fishing

In the thickly populated areas of Thailand, over-fishing has drastically reduced the number of fish. There is now a serious danger that this valuable supply of food will run out. Fish will then have to be brought from the coast. This will make fish a more expensive food for everyone.

◄ Every day a floating market is held on a *klong* just outside Bangkok. Fish, fruit, vegetables, meat and household goods are sold from the boats.

The Irrawaddy provides a cheap and convenient way of transporting teak logs from the rainforests of Burma to its sawmills, or to ports like Rangoon. ▶

Burmese River Peoples

The waters of the Irrawaddy River come from glaciers in the mountains near Burma's borders with China and India. The river then flows through rocky gorges and wooded hills until it reaches lower, drier country. There it meets Burma's other large river, the Chindwin, and flows south through Burma's oilfields and then through huge forests where teak trees grow. Finally the river spreads out into a huge delta where it meets the sea.

Homes on the Irrawaddy

The delta area of the Irrawaddy is home for a large part of Burma's population. Most of the people live in small villages built on the banks of the Irrawaddy or one of the many natural channels which carry its waters across the delta.

Burmese people build a wooden or bamboo stockade around each village. This protects the villagers against wild animals. The Burmese make their houses of wood or bamboo as well, and build them high up on piles as a protection against flooding as well as tigers, leopards, snakes and other wild animals.

Rice in the delta

The Irrawaddy delta is one of the world's major rice-growing areas, and rice is the most important agricultural product, and the main food of the Burmese. The soil in the delta is enriched every year by fertile alluvium carried down by the river.

Paddy fields

The river waters themselves are used to water the rice fields. Many of these are on islands which appear in the delta as the river level drops during the dry season. The crops are harvested before the floods of the wet season, which lasts from May to September, cause the islands to disappear again.

▲ The Irrawaddy and its tributaries drain about three-quarters of Burma. The river flows into the Bay of Bengal.

River highway

The river also provides the means of transporting the rice crop. There are few railways or good roads in Burma, and the Irrawaddy is the country's main transport route for everything. The rice is carried in small country boats down the river to the local markets.

Burma has few good roads or railways, and people have to use the small river ferry ships for even quite short journeys on the many waterways. ▼

Small ships transport the rice to the capital Rangoon. From there it is exported to Europe. The river is also used as a way of transporting giant rafts of teak logs from the rainforests. These rafts are towed by tugs down to the sea to be exported to Europe and North America. Other people use tugs to push barges carrying crude oil from the oilfields down to the refineries at Rangoon.

The growing delta

Ships can sail on the Irrawaddy for a distance of 1450 kilometres from its mouth. But the river is gradually becoming longer. This is because its delta is slowly growing in the direction of the sea because of the vast quantities of silt brought down by the river. Although the silt is good for growing rice in, it causes problems for ships since it makes the Irrawaddy continually change course. So it is difficult for all but ships with a shallow draught to sail on the river.

River Towns and Cities

Most towns and cities grew gradually from villages centred on farming. The world's first cities developed beside the large rivers on which large-scale farming depended. Villages also grew into towns and cities because, being on rivers, they were in a good position for a large number of people to trade or make a living. The rivers made it easy to transport goods.

The Île de la Cité on the River Seine is the heart of modern Paris, and was the site of the fortified island settlement from which the city grew. ▼

Market towns

Once people produced more crops or domesticated animals than they needed to feed themselves, they began to exchange or sell what they didn't need. Villages often grew if they were situated where several rivers joined.

Places like these allowed people to travel easily from over a wide area to growing market towns in order to trade. Some of the world's largest cities grew in this way, including Mannheim, Calcutta, Belgrade, Montreal and Allahabad.

River crossings

Many towns grew up by a river at a point where a bridge could be built, or at a ford where the river was shallow enough to be crossed safely on foot.

Sometimes the name of a town or city indicates that it was built at one of these river crossings, as for example Cambridge and Oxford. Other large cities built near river crossings include Frankfurt and Hamburg, both in West Germany. Berlin, the former capital of now divided Germany, also grew up on a river crossing.

Defensive sites

Some river sites had natural features which gave protection against attack in earlier days. A town built inside a large loop, or meander, in a river was safe from surprise attack from most directions because it was almost surrounded by water.

Durham and Shrewsbury in England, Besançon in France, Toledo in Spain, and Berne in Switzerland all grew up inside meanders. Islands in rivers also provided good defensive positions for towns, and both Paris, many centuries ago, and New York, more recently, began this way.

▲ An aerial view of the city of Durham in north-eastern England, which began as a walled village built on a hill inside a meander on the River Wear.

Ports

Rivers and lakes were, and in many countries still are, major routes for trade and transport. Often a town at the lowest crossing point of a river grew into a port. London and Glasgow grew in this way. Other major ports developed from villages near the sheltered mouths or estuaries of large rivers, including Southampton, Bremerhaven, Alexandria and Karachi. Another area where large ports developed was at the point furthest inland that could be reached by ships, such as Minneapolis on the Mississippi River, Kinshasa on the Zaire, and Schaffhausen on the River Rhine.

Manufacturing

Manufacturing is carried out to some extent in every town. Often, however, industry was the main reason why many river towns developed. Ship-building on the Clyde and Tyne was largely responsible for the growth of the cities on those rivers, and shipping and docks for cities on rivers at Southampton and Rotterdam.

LAKE PEOPLES

All lakes are changing because they slowly begin to fill with silt. Lake Nasser in Egypt is a huge reservoir which was formed when the Aswan High Dam was built across the River Nile. It was intended to help to protect Egypt from the Nile's yearly floods and to provide water for irrigation and hydro-electric power. When Lake Nasser was completed, it was found that most of the silt which the Nile used to leave in its delta, where it formed a fertile soil, was now being dropped to the bottom of the reservoir. Lake Nasser could perhaps completely fill with this silt. Its hydro-electric power station would then be useless, and the soil of the Nile delta would no longer be fertile.

All other lakes will in time gradually fill with silt and the villages, towns and cities which rely on them will eventually have to be abandoned. There is evidence of this having happened in the past. Long ago the area of western England known as the Somerset Levels was a huge lake. Archaeologists have unearthed the remains of 5000-year-old villages, which show that they were once occupied by people who lived by fishing in the lake and hunting wild animals in the surrounding marshes.

A more recent change is that many lakes have become tourist resorts, and the lives of the people around them are being affected by wealthy visitors. This is happening near quite small lakes, in the English Lake District and Scotland, and in large and remote lakes such as Lake Titicaca in South America.

The shores of lakes may become tourist resorts. These holidaymakers are sunning themselves by the Ossiacher Lake in Austria. ▶

◀ Sturgeons are large fish, valued for caviar, the food made from their eggs. The fish used to be caught in large numbers in the Caspian Sea, but are now in danger of being overfished.

The El Molo

The El Molo live on the barren land at the southern end of Lake Turkana in Kenya, in the East African Rift Valley. The area is hot and dry, and often years pass without rain. The name 'El Molo' means 'The people who live by catching fish'. There are a number of tribes living around the lake who catch fish, and the El Molo is the smallest of them, numbering only 400 or so. They live in tiny rounded huts which they make from a framework of sticks woven with reeds.

Log rafts and food

The people of the tribe use long poles to push themselves on fragile rafts around the shallow margins of the lake. The rafts are made of logs from *doum* palm trees which grow near the lake. The lake itself is full of many kinds of fish, and so the El Molo mostly eat fish.

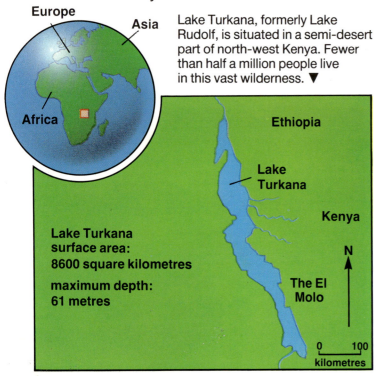

Lake Turkana, formerly Lake Rudolf, is situated in a semi-desert part of north-west Kenya. Fewer than half a million people live in this vast wilderness. ▼

Lake Turkana
surface area:
8600 square kilometres

maximum depth:
61 metres

The domed huts of a fishing village on the shores of Lake Turkana. Archaeologists discovered the remains of very early humans around the lake. ▼

Sometimes the people of the tribe cook their fish but most of the time they eat them raw. The El Molo catch their fish using nets or harpoons, and they make their nets and their ropes and lines from *doum* palm tree leaves.

Fishing on the lake

When the El Molo go fishing with a net, the whole family joins in, usually standing waist-deep in shallow water at the lakeside. They use their log rafts for harpooning fish in deeper water. They make their harpoons from hardened thorn roots.

Until recently the tips of the harpoons were made of bone. Nowadays they are made of scraps of iron heated over a dung fire and then hammered into shape. Only one or two El Molo have the skill to work iron in this way.

This fisherman is standing on the edge of the lake with his log raft beside him and his harpoon in his hand. ▼

Clay pots

Some of the tribe are also very skilful at making pots. They mould clay which they collect from the banks of the lake. The pots are shaped by hand, dried in the air and then baked over a dung fire until they are firm enough to use.

Hunting

Hippopotamuses and small crocodiles also live in the lake, and from time to time the El Molo have a change from eating fish by catching and eating a hippo or a crocodile. When the crocodiles are swimming in the lake, the El Molo spear them from rafts. Larger crocodiles bask on the lake shores, and these are hunted on foot. The hippos are killed with spears, often at night when the animals are resting in the shallows. Sometimes the El Molo also eat crocodile and turtle eggs.

The future

The El Molo are now marrying members of other tribes, and already many have begun to use basket traps to catch fish instead of catching them as they used to with nets and harpoons. The El Molo have copied these basket traps from neighbouring tribes. During the past 50 years their language has changed completely.

European missionaries are working amongst the El Molo and neighbouring tribes, a government primary school has opened, and tourism on the lake is being encouraged. The El Molo are learning ideas and customs from the world outside Lake Turkana, and are changing. They are the smallest tribe in Africa, but their marrying into other tribes may mean that they will soon no longer be a separate tribe.

The Uru

Lake Titicaca is contained in a giant hollow in the Andes Mountains in South America. It forms part of the border between Peru and Bolivia. The lake is 190 kilometres long and nearly 80 kilometres across at its widest, making it the second largest lake on the South American continent. At 3809 metres above sea-level, it is also the highest lake in the world on which steamships sail.

Lake Titicaca is fed by regular summer rains, and by streams which flow from glaciers in the mountains. The lake itself is completely surrounded by desert, but thick beds of reeds grow in its sheltered bays.

Living at high altitudes
One of the tribes of South American Indians living around Lake Titicaca is the Uru. They depend upon the lake for their food and most of their other needs. The Uru have larger hearts and lungs, and many more red blood cells than most humans. These adaptations enable them to survive in the thin, oxygen-poor air found at high altitudes.

Uru homes
Some of the Uru live on large floating rafts made of reeds from the lake shore. The others live along the lake shore. Their wooden huts are thatched with reeds, and the women also make reed mats to cover the hut floors.

Boat-building and fishing
The Uru tribesmen catch fish and also hunt birds in the reed beds around the lake. Their boats are shaped rather like large rounded canoes. Many of the boats have a large sail, and both hull and sail are woven from reeds. The boats look flimsy but are strong enough to carry passengers and animals across the lake, and they can withstand the frequent violent storms that sweep the lake.

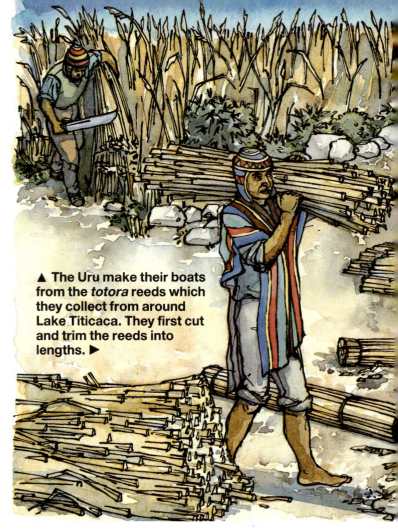

▲ The Uru make their boats from the *totora* reeds which they collect from around Lake Titicaca. They first cut and trim the reeds into lengths. ▶

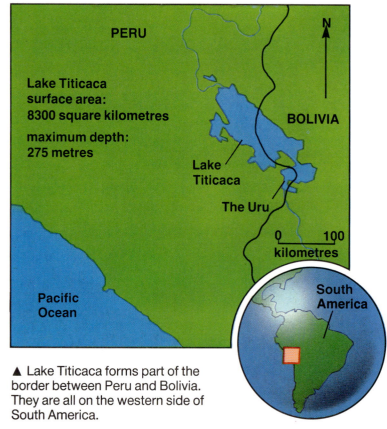

PERU

Lake Titicaca surface area: 8300 square kilometres

maximum depth: 275 metres

BOLIVIA

Lake Titicaca

The Uru

0   100
kilometres

Pacific Ocean

South America

▲ Lake Titicaca forms part of the border between Peru and Bolivia. They are all on the western side of South America.

The reeds are tied into bundles with stems of *ichu* grass which also grows around the lake. ▼

▲ The boats are often fitted with a sail, which is also made from reeds.

◄ Then parallel bundles of reeds are tied to make a long, narrow shape.

Changes

There are only a few hundred Uru people left now. Although they have their own distinctive language, most of them also speak Aymara, the language of one of the larger tribes who farm and trade around the shores of Lake Titicaca. Some Uru also speak Spanish.

Lake Titicaca has become an important commercial waterway in an area where other forms of transport are very difficult. Passengers and goods are carried across the lake by steamships which had to be brought over the Andes mountains in parts and put together on the shores of the lake. However, increasing numbers of tourists are using the steamships to visit the previously remote areas around the lake.

The Uru people have become something of an attraction for the tourists now visiting Lake Titicaca. After so much contact with, and interference from, the outside world, it seems doubtful whether the Uru can continue their traditional way of life for much longer.

▲ Uru lay out fish to dry on a floating reed island on Lake Titicaca. Behind them are two of the Uru reed-thatched houses. The Andes can be seen in the distance.

USING LAKES AND RIVERS

People, plants and animals all contain a large proportion of water. The human body, for instance, is approximately 65 per cent water, and water also forms a large part of the food we eat.

The amount of water needed to actually keep us alive is quite small – only about 2 litres a day, although more is needed in hot climates. However, this water must be clean and free from germs. Millions of the world's people have no regular supply of clean water, and so have to live all the time with a major health hazard.

As well as clean water for drinking, water is needed for washing ourselves and our clothes, for cooking and for the disposal of waste. Industry also uses vast quantities of water. Some of this water comes from wells and a little from the sea. But most comes from lakes and rivers. Unfortunately only an absolutely tiny part of the world's water is in lakes and rivers, and available for human use.

As the world population grows, the demand for water from rivers and lakes is going to increase dramatically. Many large towns and cities already use more water than is added to lakes and rivers from rainfall. In Los Angeles, the amount of water used is more than 1000 times greater than the rainfall. This means that a glass of water taken from a tap in Los Angeles may already have passed through many industrial processes and people before you drink it. This is also true of the water people drink in many cities all over the world.

50 litres per person per day

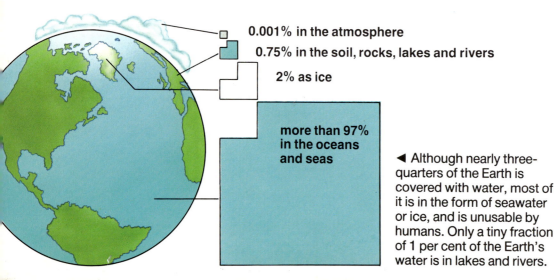

0.001% in the atmosphere

0.75% in the soil, rocks, lakes and rivers

2% as ice

more than 97% in the oceans and seas

◄ Although nearly three-quarters of the Earth is covered with water, most of it is in the form of seawater or ice, and is unusable by humans. Only a tiny fraction of 1 per cent of the Earth's water is in lakes and rivers.

◄ Paper mills like this one in Alaska are often built beside lakes or rivers. Paper-making uses up huge amounts of water because water is used to make a pulp with wood, and the paper is made from this pulp.

As countries become more industrialized, the amount of water used increases considerably. The illustration shows the amounts of water needed to make some everyday objects and to carry out some everyday activities. ▼

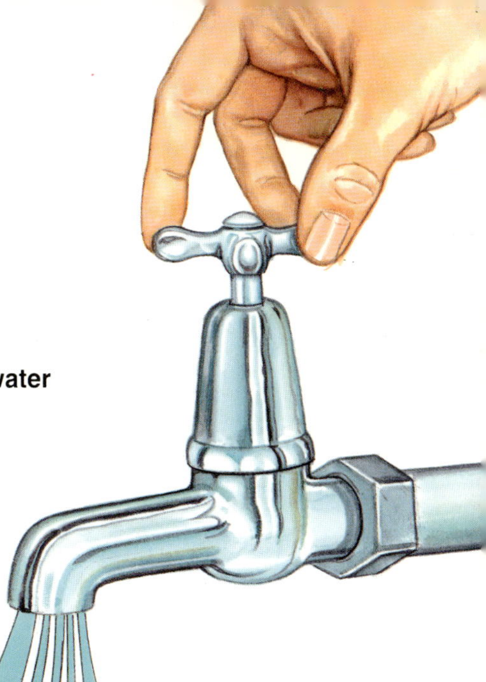

The amounts of water we use

It takes 20 000 litres of water to make 1 tonne of steel.

tyre

200 000 litres

9 litres

200 litres

sweater

Children collecting drinking water from a river in Niger, Central Africa. ▼

The Volga River

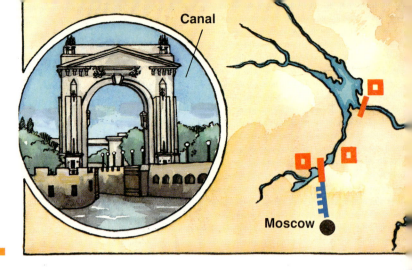

Canal

Moscow

The Volga is the longest river in Europe. It rises in marshy forests to the north-west of Moscow and flows 3690 kilometres across steppes and semi-desert regions before it finally empties into the Caspian Sea. Like most large rivers in industrialized countries, the Volga is used for many purposes besides supplying people with the fresh water they need.

Dams and flood control

On a map the Volga does not look like a river, but more like a string of lakes. These are reservoirs, which were made by building a series of huge dams across the Volga.

Each winter much of the Volga freezes over. When summer returns, the rapid thaw makes the river level rise. The Volga used to flood regularly. Now the dams and reservoirs help to regulate the flow of water, so the Volga no longer floods.

A sprinkler-type irrigation system being used to water crops on a state farm in the Engels District along the Volga valley. ▼

◀ Dairy workers on a collective farm in the Gorky region of the Volga. The women are discussing details of how much milk the cattle of this particular farm have been producing recently.

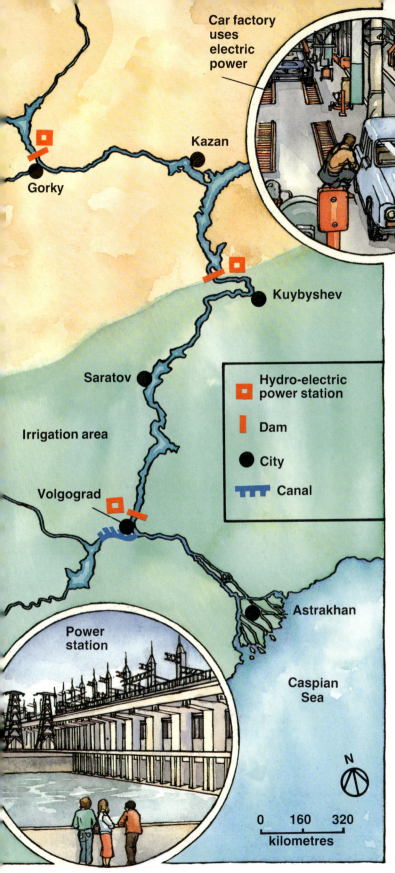

Car factory uses electric power

Gorky

Kazan

Kuybyshev

Saratov

Irrigation area

Volgograd

Hydro-electric power station

Dam

City

Canal

Power station

Astrakhan

Caspian Sea

N

0   160   320
kilometres

▲ The Volga is like a series of very large lakes. Canals link parts of the river to major cities like Moscow and Volgograd. The green area of the map shows which areas use the Volga's water for irrigation.

◄ The water from the Volga and its tributaries flows into the Caspian Sea. Europe's longest river, once feared for its annual floods, has been harnessed with the help of dams to produce hydro-electric power, while ships can sail 3000 kilometres from Moscow to Volgograd.

Freedom from drought

The Volga flows into desert and semi-desert land as it nears the Caspian Sea. The people in these areas suffered severe droughts in 1924 and again in 1984. Here the river water is used mostly for irrigation in fields. Irrigation can increase plant growth as much as six times and almost completely removes the threat of drought. There can be problems, however. As the irrigation water evaporates, salt builds up in the soil. Eventually crops can no longer grow because the soil is too saturated in salt.

A transport highway

The fisheries of the Volga were once important, particularly for sturgeon, the fish from which caviar is prepared. Now the river water is polluted, there are far fewer fish, and much less work for the fisheries. The use of the Volga for carrying goods and people is, however, increasing in a consistent way.

This is not surprising, because canals link the Volga not only to the Baltic and White Seas to the west and north, but also to the Mediterranean, by way of the Black Sea, in the south. In these ways the Volga crosses a large part of Russia.

The Volga rafts

Timber is by far the most frequently carried cargo along the Volga. There are giant timber rafts from the northern forests of Russia all along the river.

Often a whole family will look after one of these rafts, and live for months at a time on the raft in a log cabin. When the raft reaches its destination, Astrakhan on the Volga delta, the timber is loaded onto ships for export to Western Europe. The family then travels back up river on a passenger boat, to collect another raft.

Changing Waters

Many towns, cities and factories were built near rivers or lakes so that people could make use of the water. Unfortunately, the people often return the used water to the lake or river only after they have mixed it with chemicals and waste of different kinds.

Pollution

Industrial wastes, untreated sewage and other poisons have polluted many lakes and rivers. These substances can kill all living things and make the water unfit for human use. A dramatic example of pollution occurred on the River Rhine, by accident, in November 1986. While firemen were fighting a fire at a chemical factory near Basle in Switzerland, water polluted with a mixture of 34 different chemicals poured into the Rhine. Millions of fish were killed. The waters of the Rhine were unfit for human use. Scientists believe it may be 10 years before the fish return.

Small boats like these travel in Bangladesh to the markets in the scattered communities so often affected by floods. ▼

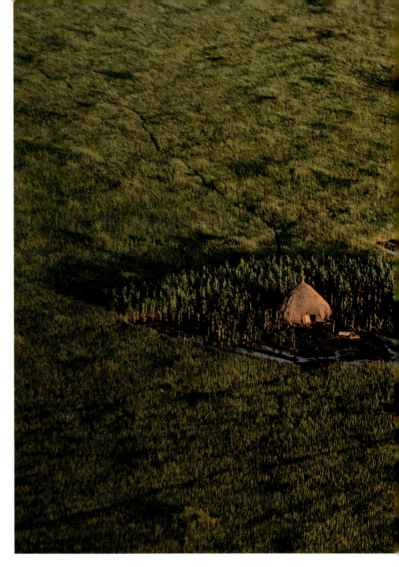

Some factories collect their polluted water in reservoirs and clean it before releasing it back into the river. ▼

Acid rain

The biggest threat to many rivers and lakes at the moment is from 'acid rain'. Fossil fuels such as oil and petrol release the gases sulphur dioxide and nitrogen dioxide into the air when they are burnt. These gases dissolve in water in the atmosphere and produce an acid rain that may fall huge distances from where the pollution was first formed. Already fish are dying in lakes and rivers in Scotland, Wales and North America, while in Scandinavia many lakes and rivers have no life in them because of acid rain.

Flooding and soil erosion

Many rivers flood, often causing serious damage and loss of life. In some cases, the flooding may be due to people having cut down trees at a point farther up the river.

In Nepal, villagers have cleared large areas of forest for firewood. Now, when it rains, the soil is easily washed away, ruining the fields in Nepal.

▲ An aerial view of one of the villages of the Dinka people in the Sudd in Sudan, north-east Africa.

This chokes rivers with silt. Some scientists say that this may be causing floods hundreds of miles away, in the lowlands of Bangladesh and India.

Threatened livelihoods

In Africa over half a million people in Uganda, Kenya and Tanzania depend on fish from Lake Victoria. Some of the smaller fish species are facing extinction because of over-fishing in the shallows. The three governments plan to modernize the fisheries and concentrate on the deeper water fish, but thousands will lose jobs.

The Dinka people who live in the swampy area known as the Sudd in Sudan have a different problem. Egypt, Sudan's northern neighbour, wants to drain water from part of the Sudd into the River Nile. The Dinka will lose their traditional way of life as the area dries out.

The Future

The lives of many of the river and lake peoples are changing. They have little or no say in these changes. In the developed countries there is a growing demand for lakes and rivers to be used for sports and leisure activities such as swimming, sailing, rowing, canoeing and water-skiing.

Peace and quiet

In Europe and much of North America, the most popular river or lake sport is fishing. Even more people are happy to walk or picnic by rivers and lakes. The banks of rivers and lakes in or near towns and cities are often one of the few places where people can enjoy peace and quiet.

Cruises along rivers such as the Nile offer tourists a chance to see new ways of life and to visit historic sites, such as the Pyramids, at the same time. ▼

Floating hotels

The need to 'get away from it all' can also be seen in the growing use of lakes and rivers for holiday cruises. A large number of floating hotels carry tourists along the River Rhine and its tributary the Moselle, and also along the Nile. The tourists can enjoy the dramatic scenery, historic towns and ancient monuments along the river banks, while relaxing in comfort. Holidays of this kind can also be very beneficial for health.

Lake tourism

Lakes, too, have their tourist cruises and some of them, including the English Lake District, the Scottish lochs, Lake Lucerne in Switzerland, the Great Lakes in North America and even the remote Lake Titicaca in South America have tourist resorts on their shores. People use the resorts as bases and take boat trips on the lakes.

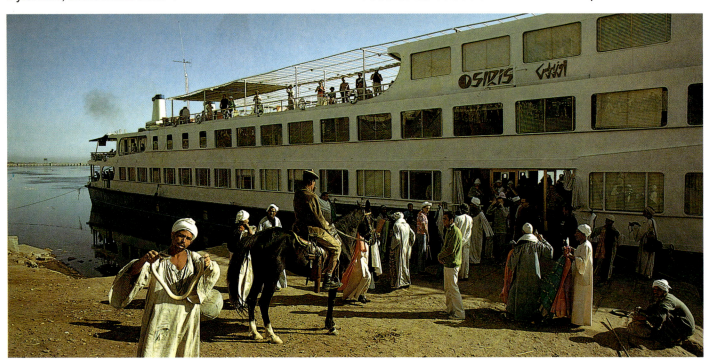

Cleaning-up lakes and rivers

All of the sporting and leisure activities cause some disturbance to and interference with the lives of the river and lake peoples. Fortunately there is a benefit. Sport and recreation both need clean water.

Some governments are so worried about the polluted state of their rivers and lakes that they are trying to repair the damage of the past. By the late 1950s almost nothing could live in the River Thames. Now many of London's old docks have been closed, and new sewage works built.

Factories now have to pass their wastes through sewage works instead of dumping them straight into the Thames. Because the water is now cleaner, fish, birds and many other forms of wildlife have returned to the river.

▲ Windsurfers on the Silser Lake in south-east Switzerland. This form of sailing has become a world-wide popular water sport since the early 1970s.

Fragile lakes and rivers

It has to be remembered, though, that a river or lake is fragile. Once cleaned up, it can still be easily damaged again. As recently as the 1960s, one of Europe's best known rivers, the Rhine, was little better than a sewer in which no living thing survived and in which people would not swim.

Attempts to limit the pollution were taking effect, and the water quality was improving, when chemical spillage in 1986 killed most of the fish and made the water unusable again. There are industrial sites on the banks of many of the world's rivers, and each can cause just as much damage as the Basle plant did to the Rhine.

Books and Places

Books to read

The Young Geographer Investigates: Rivers, Terry Jennings, OUP 1986
Visual Science: Water, Bill Gunston, Macdonald 1980
Rivers of the World Series, including **The Amazon**, **The Congo**, **The Ganges**, **The Nile**, **The Rhine** and **The Volga** Wayland.
Nature's Landscapes: Rivers and People, Tom Browne, Wayland 1985
The Family Water Naturalist, Heather Angel and Pat Wolseley, Michael Joseph 1982
Rivers and Lakes, Martyn Bramwell, Franklin Watts 1986

There are two main kinds of freshwater fishing: game fishing and coarse fishing. ▼

Places to visit

There are boat trips from several capital cities, including London, Amsterdam and Paris, which will show you the ways in which a city makes use of its river.

It might be possible to visit your local waterworks or water control authority. You can find the address in the telephone directory.

Questions for you to think about

Where is your local reservoir? How big is it? Is it used for water sports, angling, or other leisure activities?

Is there a major power station in your area? Is it a hydro-electric power station? If not, does it use water for cooling or to produce steam to turn its generators?

Museums

You can learn about river and lake peoples by visiting anthropological museums, such as the Museum of Mankind in London, or the Museum of the American Indian in New York.

A few museums specialize in the boats used on inland waterways such as lakes, rivers and canals. The Boat Museum at Ellesmere Port, Cheshire, England, has the largest such boat collection in Europe. You can also visit the Exeter Maritime Museum, England.

Study your local river

Choose a river near your home or school and make a study of it. Look at a map of the river. Trace it and mark on it any towns or villages along the course of the river.

What uses do these towns and villages make of the river and its water? Where is the river's source? Where is the mouth of the river? Is there a port? If so, what cargoes does it handle?

Find out by asking anglers what fish are found in the river. What other sports or leisure activities is the river used for? Is the river polluted? If so, what has caused the pollution, and is there any local concern about it?

The five longest rivers and five largest lakes

River	Location	Length (kilometres)	Area of drainage basin (square kilometres)
Nile	North-East Africa	6671	2867000
Amazon	South America	6280	7050000
Mississippi-Missouri	North America	6019	3221000
Ob-Irtysh	USSR	5410	2975000
Yangzi	China	6300	1807000

Lake	Location	Surface Area (square kilometres)	Depth (metres)
Caspian Sea	USSR/Iran	371000	1025
Superior	North America	82414	406
Victoria	Africa	68100	80
Aral Sea	USSR	66500	68
Huron	North America	59596	229

Source: Mitchell Beazley Great Geographical Atlas 1982

'Whitewater' canoeing near an Austrian waterfall. White water is the term used for the often very rough river waters around rapids or waterfalls. ▶

Events

1482 The Portuguese Diogo Cão discovered the mouth of the Zaire River.

1500 Amazon River first seen by Spaniard, Vincente Pinzon.

1535 The French explorer Jacques Cartier sailed up the St. Lawrence River into the interior of North America.

1541 The Amazon River was explored, by accident, by the Spaniard, Francisco de Orellana.

1638 Pedro Teixeira explored the main course of the Amazon.

1681 Robert La Salle claimed the whole valley of the Mississippi River for France.

1794–1805 The Scottish explorer Mungo Park explored the River Niger.

1828–36 The course of the Murray River, Australia, was traced by Charles Stuart and Thomas Mitchell.

1855 David Livingstone discovered the Victoria Falls.

1858 John Speke discovered Lake Victoria.

1863 The source of the River Nile was discovered by J. H. Speke and J. A. Grant.

1876–77 H. M. Stanley explored the Zaire River.

1974 John Blashford-Snell led the first expedition to complete a full navigation of the Zaire River.

Word List

Acid rain Pollution caused by waste substances in the atmosphere forming weak acids in rain water.

Alluvium Soil moved and deposited by a river or stream.

Archaeologist A scientist who studies the ancient remains of people who lived long ago.

Canal An artificial waterway.

Dam A wall or barrier built across a river.

Delta A fan-shaped area of land where a river or stream divides as it approaches sea level. It is formed by deposits of alluvium.

Equator The imaginary line around the centre of the Earth, where the climate is usually hot.

Estuary The wide mouth of a river where the river currents meet the sea tides.

Evaporation Heat or moving air changing a liquid into a vapour.

Floodplain Part of a river valley which is covered by alluvium spread by the river when it floods.

Ford A shallow place in a river where it is possible to wade or drive across.

Gorge A deep narrow valley with steep rocky sides.

Harpoon A spear, attached to a rope, for catching fish.

Hydro-electric power Electric power produced by moving water which turns generators, usually in a power station at a dam.

Irrigation An artificial way of watering the land by carrying water through channels, or in containers, from rivers.

Klong The Thai people's name for the canals they live on and around.

Mandioca An important food plant, also known as cassava or manioc.

Meander A bend or loop in the course of a river.

Paddy fields Rice fields.

Plain A large stretch of flat country, usually lowland.

Plateau A high but mainly flat area of land.

Pollution The contamination of lakes, rivers, seas, the air and the land, through human activities.

Rainforest Dense forests found in areas close to the Equator.

Rapids Fast-flowing and often rocky stretches of a river, caused by a steep slope or a sudden narrowing of the river's course.

Reservoir An artificial lake for storing water.

Rift valley A valley formed when the land sinks between two roughly parallel faults.

River basin The area of land from which the water of a river and its tributaries is drawn. Also known as a drainage basin.

Sewage Waste material and liquid from factories and houses, carried away by drains or sewers.

Silt Alluvium which is finer than sand carried by moving water.

Soil erosion The gradual removal of topsoil from an area of land by the action of flowing water, rain or wind.

Source The place from which a stream or river starts.

Spring A flow of water from the ground.

Steppes A term applied to the open treeless grass plains in the Soviet Union.

Tributary A stream or river that flows into a larger river.

Tropics The warm regions of the Earth on either side of the Equator where, at midsummer, the sun is directly overhead.

Well A hole in the ground through which water or oil are raised to the surface.

Index

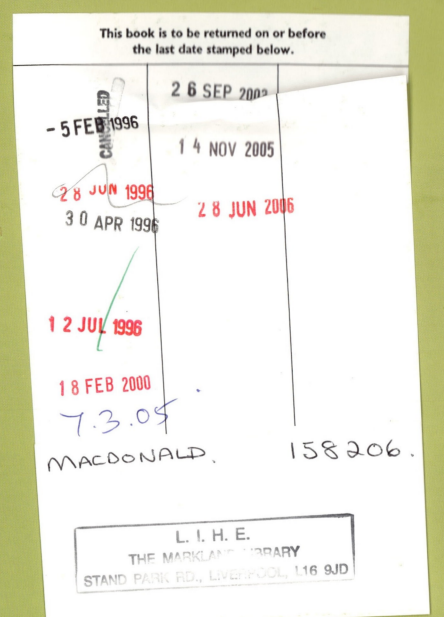

This book is to be returned on or before
the last date stamped below.